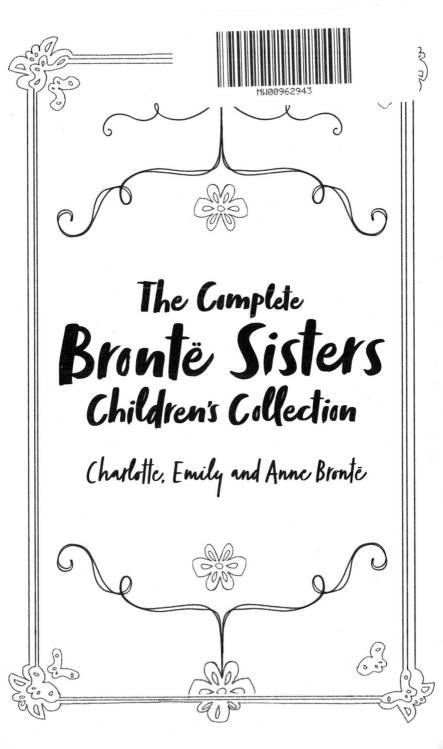

The Complete
Brontë Sisters
Children's Collection

Charlotte, Emily and Anne Brontë

Published by Sweet Cherry Publishing Limited
Unit 36, Vulcan House,
Vulcan Road,
Leicester, LE5 3EF
United Kingdom

First published in the UK in 2022
2022 edition

2 4 6 8 10 9 7 5 3 1

ISBN: 978-1-78226-712-6

© Sweet Cherry Publishing

The Complete Brontë Sisters Children's Collection:
The Life of the Brontë Sisters

Cover design by Arianna Bellucci and Amy Booth
Illustrations by Arianna Bellucci

Lexile® code numerical measure L = Lexile® 840L

www.sweetcherrypublishing.com

Printed and bound in Turkey
T.OP005

The Life of the Brontë Sisters

Stephanie Baudet

Sweet
Cherry

Dear Reader,

The Brontë sisters wrote stories that have been loved by many for centuries, but their own stories deserve to be told too. All of the events in this book really happened, and the letters and diary entries included within these pages are very similar to those the sisters wrote in real life.

This is the remarkable story of Charlotte, Emily and Anne.

Aunt Elizabeth Branwell

Born 1776
Died 1842

Maria Branwell

Born 1783
Died 1821

Patrick Bronte

Born 1777
Died 1861

m.

Maria

Born 1814
Died 1825

Elizabeth

Born 1815
Died 1825

Charlotte

Born 1816
Died 1855

Keeper

Flossy

Hero

Branwell

Born 1817
Died 1848

Emily

Born 1818
Died 1848

Anne

Born 1820
Died 1849

Chapter One

The Parsonage, Haworth   September 1821

My dear Elizabeth,

I regret to tell you that your sister, my beloved wife, passed away today. Our six little children are very sad, but I must not neglect my work as curate in the church.

Could you to come and look after them? We have three servants to help you.

Yours,

Patrick Brontë

The next day, Elizabeth Branwell stepped onto the stage coach at Penzance, in Cornwall, for the long journey north to Yorkshire. She would end up staying there for over twenty years.

Aunt Branwell was forty-five years old. She had never wanted to marry, which would have meant giving all her money to her husband. She liked living independently and doing as she wanted.

As her horse and cart rattled up the steep cobblestoned road in Haworth village, she wondered whether she had made the right decision. The village sat on a hill at the edge of the Pennine moors, exposed to the harsh weather. It was very different to Penzance.

As well as the cold wind, there was a nasty smell. There were two public toilets on the main street and the cesspits beneath them often overflowed into the street.

The Parsonage, where the Brontës lived, was not much better. The well from which all their water came was very near a large graveyard.

Patrick Brontë was worried about the high number of cholera cases and other diseases in the village. The average age of death in

Haworth was nineteen, and half of the children born there died before they were six years old.

When Aunt Branwell arrived at her brother-in-law's house, she was greeted by his children:

Maria, aged eight, Elizabeth, aged seven, Charlotte, aged five, Branwell, aged four, Emily, aged three, and Anne, aged eight months.

Aunt Branwell was not used to children. But, kindly and bravely, she took on the job of raising them.

The Parsonage, Haworth   September 1821

My dear Gwen,

I have arrived safely in Haworth. It is such a quiet, isolated place. But the moors are beautiful.

Already I miss my beloved Cornwall, with its warm weather, and my good friends, like yourself. But it is my duty to stay and care for the family. Poor Patrick and the little ones are heartbroken at the loss of Maria.

I look forward to your letters.

Yours,

Elizabeth Branwell

Chapter Two

For the first few years, Aunt Branwell taught the children. They learnt to sew and mend. They read newspapers and magazines and talked to Papa and Aunt about what was going on in the world.

In 1824, Patrick Brontë saw an advertisement for a school that taught daughters of church clergymen like him. It was at Cowan Bridge, about fifty miles from Haworth. The cost was fourteen pounds per year for each pupil, and the rest of the fees were paid by generous donations from rich people.

At the end of the summer, the four eldest girls went to the school. It was a low building, with a space divided into little flowerbeds where the pupils could grow vegetables.

There were no holidays for the pupils apart from in the summer. They didn't even have holidays at Christmas!

Charlotte wrote a letter home.

September 1824

Dear Papa, Aunt, Anne and Branwell,

We have settled in very well at school. We are enjoying the lessons and have made friends with the other girls. We do miss you all but are grateful for the opportunity to have an education, especially as we are girls.

Love,

Charlotte

This is what she would have written if she were telling the truth.

September 1824

Dear Papa, Aunt, Anne and Branwell,
It is horrible here. The older girls are terrible bullies and we have very little to eat. The breakfast porridge is nearly always burnt.

The teachers are cruel too. You know that Maria is very good at history, but the teacher, Miss Taylor, dislikes her and marks her bottom of the class. She sometimes hangs a sign around her neck that says "Slattern". We do not know what this means, but it must be something horrible.
Wishing we were back home,
Charlotte

During her time at the school, Charlotte also kept a diary, which she hid under her thin mattress. She would have been in big trouble if it had been found, but writing in it helped her cope with her troubles and worries.

November 1824

Winter begins. The bell rings
before dawn and we get up to wash.
Sometimes the water is frozen.

On Sundays we walk three miles to
the cold church in our thin clothes. Our
feet stay wet all day long.

Maria's cough is getting worse. I am
really worried about her.

A few months later, Patrick
Brontë received a letter from
Cowan Bridge School.

Cowan Bridge School   February 1825

Dear Mr Brontë,

I regret that your daughter, Maria, is very ill. Please come at once to take her home. I can no longer be responsible for her.

Sincerely,

Miss Evans

Headmistress

The daffodils were in full bloom when Maria was brought home to the Parsonage. It was her favourite time of year, but she was too ill to notice the spring flowers beginning to shoot. Charlotte, Elizabeth and Emily left the school at the same

time, and the family prepared themselves to say goodbye to their big sister.

Maria died three months later, aged eleven.

Their sister, Elizabeth, became ill too. She died six weeks later, at the age of ten. Both had tuberculosis.

Suddenly the house seemed very empty.

Charlotte and Emily did not return to the cold, harsh school.

Chapter Three

June 1826

It is more than a year since we lost our dear sisters, but I can sometimes hear their laughter when the house is quiet and the wind whistles through the eves.

We have all been kept busy writing poems and stories. Branwell calls this 'scribblemania'!

Papa has recently been to Leeds and brought us back a present each. I have a model farm, Emily has wooden animals, Anne has model people and Branwell has a set of twelve wooden soldiers. We have each chosen a soldier and given him a name. Mine is called the Duke of Wellington.

We are building a land called Angria for all of our people to live in.

The children continued to create their imaginary land and its people for many years, even into adulthood. They wrote plays for the characters, drew maps and made tiny books the size of

matchboxes, with miniscule writing and drawings inside.

Life in the Parsonage went on as usual for the next four years. However, in 1830, Patrick became very ill. He had a lung condition that often made him poorly, but it had never been this bad before.

After weeks of rest, Patrick began to recover. He then received a letter from his old friends, the Reverend Thomas and Mrs Atkinson.

Dewsbury,   July 1830

My dear Patrick,

We are so glad to receive news that you have recovered from your illness. You must have been worried about your children. If you had been unable to work, you would have lost the house and all been homeless.

The girls and Branwell must be able to earn their own living, to protect them in case this should happen again.

Since we are her godparents, we would like to help by paying for Charlotte to go to a very good school, called Roe Head.

We hope you will accept our offer.

Sincerely,

Rev Thomas and Mrs Atkinson

Charlotte was delighted to go to the school. It didn't take long to pack her small bag for the twenty-mile journey. Nevertheless, it was daunting for her to go alone. The school had a friendly atmosphere, but she was so used to being around her siblings that she couldn't help feeling a little afraid.

Roe Head School   September 1830

Dear Papa, Aunt and everyone,

I am grateful to the Atkinsons for giving me this opportunity, but I did cry as I stood outside this great rambling house, watching the wagon that had brought me here pull away. I feel so lonely and miss you all. And it is so obvious that I am poor! The girls have noticed my drab, faded, old-fashioned clothes.

But the sisters who run the school, the Miss Woolers, are kind ladies and good teachers. They encourage everyone to join in during discussions and give their points of view. We are well fed and looked after. It is so much better here than Cowan Bridge School!

Please write soon.

Love,

Charlotte

October 1830

Dear All,

I have made two wonderful friends!
They are new girls too. They are called
Ellen Nussey and Mary Taylor. I was a
little unhappy and lonely before, but not
anymore.

Love,

Charlotte

Charlotte stayed at Roe Head
for a year and a half. Although she
was quite shy, she was respected

and liked by the teachers and other pupils.

Charlotte continued to write to her friend, Ellen, even after she had left the school.

The Parsonage, Haworth   November 1832

Dear Ellen,

You asked me to tell you what I do all day since I left the school.

In the mornings, from nine until half past twelve, I teach my sisters. Then we walk until dinner time. After dinner I sew until teatime. After tea I either read, write, do some embroidery, draw or do whatever I want!

I can't wait to hear your news, too.

Love,

Charlotte

The two girls would remain best friends for life.

Chapter Four

In 1835, when Charlotte was
nineteen, she was invited back to Roe
Head School to work as a teacher.
Part of her salary paid for Emily, the
second oldest sibling, to attend the
school. But Emily only stayed there
for three months. She was a very

nervous girl, and missed her family, her pets, and the freedom and comfort of her beloved moors. She quickly became very ill with homesickness.

So Emily returned home and Anne, the youngest, went instead. This was Anne's first time away from home, and the gentle, quiet girl also felt very homesick. But, despite this, she was determined to get an education so that she could support herself. She worked hard, eventually earning herself a good-conduct medal.

PRIZE FOR GOOD CONDUCT

PRESENTED TO

Miss A. Brontë

WITH MISS WOOLER'S KIND LOVE, ROE HEAD.

DEC. 14TH 1836

Then suddenly, Anne became very ill with stomach pain, and the asthma she had suffered from all her life became worse.

In one of her letters to Ellen, Charlotte wrote:

I am very worried about Anne. It makes me miserable to see her in pain and having difficulty breathing. Miss Wooler thinks I am making a fuss over nothing. I got cross and told her what had happened to Maria and Elizabeth.

At Charlotte's insistence, Miss Wooler wrote to Patrick about Anne's illness. Although she didn't want to leave school, her father took her home to rest.

Charlotte stayed on as a teacher until early 1837. She was still a bit shy, but was now a strong, independent woman of twenty-one.

During this time, the sisters'
brother, Branwell, had shown talent
as a portrait artist. His father and
aunt paid for him to go to the Royal
Academy in London, but he had lacked
the courage to even enter the building.
Instead, he'd spent all the money he
had on partying and gambling.

No matter where they were, or what
they were doing, all of the sisters
wrote poetry in their spare time.

Once, Charlotte wrote a letter to a very famous poet named Robert Southey.

The Parsonage, Haworth   January 1838

Dear Mr Southey,

I am a great admirer of your work. I write poetry too, although in a small way. It gives me much pleasure.

I have enclosed two poems that I would be honoured to have you read and advise upon.

Yours sincerely,

Charlotte Brontë

His pompous reply angered Charlotte, although it did not surprise her. The young women were used to being put down by men, who didn't think that women could achieve what men did.

January 1838

Dear Miss Brontë,

I always tell any male poets who ask my advice that it is difficult to earn either a living or fame from writing poetry.

As a woman, you stand even less chance.

Sincerely,

Robert Southey

Charlotte boldly wrote back to Southey. She explained that she never neglected the duties that were expected of her, such as teaching or sewing, but she preferred to write and would continue to do so for as long as she pleased.

That same year, Charlotte received a proposal of marriage from Henry, her friend Ellen's brother.

June 1838

My dear Miss Brontë,

In my work as a church minister I am in need of a wife by my side, to help look after my pupils and work with me for the greater glory of God.

It would bring me great pleasure if you could be that wife.

May I come and ask your father for his permission?

Yours,

Henry Nussey

It was a very unromantic proposal. Charlotte knew that a lot of marriages weren't based on love, but she turned him down anyway. Henry didn't really know her at all. She was very different from this serious man and she would never change who she was for someone else.

Chapter Five

In 1838, Branwell found a job as
a clerk at a newly opened railway
station near Halifax. He had no real
interest in railways, but it was a good
secure job. Branwell's father thought
that his son's talents were wasted in
such a job. He wished that Branwell

would earn lots of money and a good reputation through his art.

For Branwell's sisters, there were very few jobs available. They had the choice of being a servant in a big house or of working in a factory, which could be dangerous with their machinery. Fortunately, as they were well-educated, the sisters also had the choice of being a governess or teacher.

Charlotte and Anne both got jobs as governesses. Emily stayed at home to look after Aunt and Papa,

who were getting older and needed
more help than they used to. Here
she felt most comfortable and useful.

Anne wrote to Charlotte about her new position.

Mirfield   September 1839

Dear Charlotte,

I am in charge of two children — Joshua and Mary Ingham, aged six and five. They are very badly behaved, being more like wild animals than children!

They have been taught no manners at all, and are cruel to their animals. They treat me much the same.

I hope that you are getting on better than I, dear sister.

With love,

Anne

Unfortunately, Charlotte's pupils were not much better than Anne's. Their mother treated Charlotte like dirt under her feet. She left the job at the end of the term, but Anne was determined to complete the year.

Once the long year was up, Anne put an advertisement in the paper.

Experienced governess looking for position.
Teaches music, singing, drawing, French, Latin and German.
Salary required: £50 per annum.
Please write to: Miss A. Brontë, The Parsonage, Haworth, Yorkshire.

Anne received only one reply. It came from a Reverend Robinson of Little Ouseburn, near York – seventy miles from her home.

The Robinsons were very snobbish and treated their servants badly, but Anne accepted the position and stayed for five years. Unlike her previous pupils, Anne could see that Lydia, Elizabeth and Mary could be taught the things that she believed really mattered: honesty, kindness and respect for themselves and others.

Meanwhile, Charlotte's old school friend, Mary Taylor, had moved to Brussels with her brother, Joe.

Brussels   January 1842

Dear Charlotte,

We are so enjoying Brussels! There are so many wonderful sights to see, especially the cathedral of Saint Michael and Sainte Gudula.

I wish you could come and see for yourself. You would be welcome to stay with us, of course.

Your friend,

Mary

Charlotte was excited by the idea of going to Brussels. Quickly, she wrote to her aunt.

Rawdon   January 1842

Dear Aunt Branwell,

I have received a letter from my friend, Mary Taylor, in Brussels. She has invited me to go and stay with her. I would love to attend a finishing school there to help me prepare for running our own school one day. You know this has always been a dream of mine and my sisters.

Perhaps Emily would like to come, too!

If you could kindly let me have one hundred pounds, I will go immediately.

I would be so grateful for your help, Aunt.

Your loving niece,

Charlotte

Charlotte's aunt did not refuse. In February 1842, both Charlotte and Emily set out for Brussels.

Chapter Six

Pensionnat Heger,   March 1842

Rue d'Isabel,

Brussels

Dear Ellen,

Here we are in Brussels! Emily and I
have found a very good school run by a
young couple, Monsieur and Madame
Heger. Monsieur Heger is a very
gifted teacher. In return for our board

and lodging, I am teaching English and
Emily is teaching music.

Father has promised to look after
Emily's hawk, Hero, while we are
away. She does love that bird.
Love,
Charlotte

Both Charlotte and Emily settled
into their life at the school, but their
happiness did not last long. At the
beginning of April, they received a shock
in the form of a letter from their father.

The Parsonage, Haworth   June 1842

My dear Charlotte and Emily,

I am writing to tell you about Branwell.
He was careless about his work on the
railway and has been dismissed from his
job. Since then, Anne has found him a job
as tutor to the Robinson boy. He will be
starting there at the end of September.

There is another thing I must tell you,
Emily. I regret that Branwell has lost
your hawk. He tried to teach him to hunt
like a falcon and he flew away.

Your father,
Patrick Brontë

Emily was heartbroken over Hero. She loved all animals, but her merlin hawk was very special to her, ever since she had found him injured on the moor and nursed him back to health.

Back in England, at the Robinsons' house, Anne received a letter from Branwell one morning. She kept it in her pocket all day so that she could read it when her work was done in the evening.

The Parsonage, Haworth   September 1842

My dear Anne,

I must give you some bad news.

One of our curates who helps Father,

Willy Weightman, died yesterday.

You know how good he was at visiting

the sick people in the village, and

there is cholera about at present. He

quickly fell ill.

I know you were fond of him.

Love,

Branwell

Anne sat holding the letter, failing to hold back her tears.

Of the several curates Patrick had to assist him over the years, Willy was the best. The sisters had known him since they were

young, and everyone in the village had loved his humour and bright outlook on life.

In 1840, when he had discovered that none of the girls had ever received a Valentine, Willy trudged ten miles to Bradford to send them each a Valentine card with poems in them written by himself. He did not sign his name on them, but all of the sisters guessed who they had been from. Happily, they wrote back to him:

We cannot write or talk like you;
We're plain folks every one;
You've played a clever trick on us,
We thank you for the fun.
Believe us frankly when we say
(Our words though blunt are true).
At home, abroad, by night or day,
We all wish well to you.

But Anne had been fonder
of Willy than anyone. She had
secretly hoped that one day they
could be together and marry. Now
any chance of that was gone.

After his death, her poems
became about him.

Yes, thou art gone, and never more
Thy sunny smile shall gladden me.
But I may pass the old church door
And pace the floor that covers thee.

Not long after, Charlotte and
Emily received another sad
letter from their father – this one
bringing the worst news of all.

The Parsonage, Haworth   October 1842

My dear Charlotte and Emily,

I regret that your aunt has been taken
ill. Please come home at once.

Fondest love,

Papa

Charlotte and Emily packed
their bags as quickly as they could,
but before they could leave the next
day, another letter arrived.

Their aunt was dead. She was
sixty-six years old.

Chapter Seven

The family was devastated by Aunt Branwell's death. The loss was felt even more so by Charlotte and Emily, who arrived home too late to attend her funeral and say their goodbyes. The house seemed empty without her strong presence.

In January 1843, Charlotte travelled alone back to Brussels. Emily felt that she needed to stay at home to look after their father, who was not in good health and whose eyesight was worsening.

Upon Charlotte's return, Monsieur Heger asked her to teach him English. While he was often irritable, Charlotte had become very fond of the man. She couldn't help but be attracted to how passionate he was about teaching.

On his birthday, she wanted to give him a silk watch pouch that she had made, but she knew she that could not give such a special gift to a married man. So, she gave him the usual posy that all the students

gave, made of coloured leaves with a red rosebud in the middle.

Charlotte stayed at the school for another year but became more and more unhappy. Everyone knew that she had fallen in love with Monsieur Heger. At last, when she thought that her heart could take it no longer, she decided to leave.

With Anne and Branwell away and aunt gone, Charlotte thought she should stay at home and help Emily with the household tasks.

Over the coming months, Charlotte wrote Monsieur Heger many letters.

I cannot lose your friendship. Give me just a little hope. Then I shall be happy. I shall have a reason for living.

But Monsieur Heger only replied to her once or twice. Then, his letters stopped altogether.

In July 1845, Branwell found himself in trouble again. He lost his job as tutor at the Robinsons' because he'd had a romantic affair with Mrs Robinson.

He was very unhappy. In the depths of depression, he became weak, refusing to eat.

Because of Branwell's disgrace, Anne also left the Robinsons'. Saddened that they would no longer get to see her, one of her pupils gave Anne the present of a King Charles spaniel puppy called Flossy.

It was at this sad and uncertain time that all three of the young Brontë women began writing their novels.

Chapter Eight

Anne began writing *Agnes Grey*, inspired by her work as a governess, being challenged by difficult pupils. Charlotte began writing *The Professor*, drawing on her experience as a teacher in Brussels. And Emily began writing *Wuthering Heights*, with a background of the wild moors that she loved so much.

The girls walked around the dining room table every evening, arm in arm, discussing what they had written that day. But they kept their writing a secret from everyone else. Charlotte never even told her close friend, Ellen Nussey.

One day, the three young women decided to put some of their best poems into a book together and have it published, even though they had to pay for it them themselves.

They knew that people would probably not buy or read the poems if they knew they were written by women, so they invented new author names for themselves. Charlotte became *Currer Bell*, Emily became *Ellis Bell* and Anne became *Acton Bell*. They chose the name Bell after their father's newest curate, Arthur Bell Nicholls.

The book sold only three copies but
the sisters were not too disappointed.

They were delighted just to see their first works printed.

Meanwhile, they made plans to open their very own school. They made advertisements and put them in as many newspapers as they could.

Then they waited.

No pupils came. Charlotte thought perhaps it was just as well, because there wasn't much room in the Parsonage, and being next to a graveyard was not inviting.

Eventually, the sisters three decided that they must be content with the fact that they had at least tried.

After more than a year of hard work, all three of the sisters' books were finished. They anxiously sent them to a publisher.

The Parsonage, Haworth   April 1846

Aylott and Jones,
Publishers

Dear Gentlemen,

C, E, and A. Bell have each written a tale of fiction.

We hope that, after you have read them, you will think them good enough for publication.

Yours sincerely,
Currer Bell

They were rejected. Refusing to give up, Charlotte got together a list of publishers and sent them out again and again. It seemed that they would never succeed.

Then, in
August 1846,
Wuthering Heights and *Agnes Grey*
found publishers. Emily and Anne
would have to pay fifty pounds
each to publish them. They both
used money that their Aunt had
left them when she died. They
knew that she would be happy they
were pursuing their dreams.

Charlotte continued to send
The Professor to other publishers,
never giving up hope. Finally, she

sent it to Smith, Elder & Co. She had a reply in two weeks. They did not want to publish the book, but they said that if she could write something else they would be happy to consider it.

By that time, their father, Patrick, was almost completely blind. Emily and Charlotte travelled to Manchester to find a surgeon who could perform an operation to help.

On 25th August 1846, the operation was performed.

Afterwards, Patrick recovered
in Manchester, with the care of
Charlotte and a nurse. He had to lie
flat in a dark room for a month with
bandages over his eyes.

Boundary Street,   September 1846

Manchester

Dear Emily,

Father is recovering well. He can almost

read and write again! Although I am

a little bored, I have begun writing a

new book called Jane Eyre, so that is

occupying my thoughts.

    We shall be home in another two

weeks.

    Give our love to Anne and Branwell,

as well as the servants.

Love,

Charlotte (and Papa)

When they arrived home, they found that Branwell was feeling worse. While Patrick felt better than ever, and continued his work in the church, Branwell became more and more depressed, despite his sisters' encouragement. Then, to make matters worse, Branwell fell very ill.

Chapter Nine

More than a year later, *Agnes
Grey* and *Wuthering Heights*
were still not published. First, the
publishers had said that some of the
pages were lost. Then, something
went wrong at the printers. The
publishers did not answer Anne and

Emily's letters. Months went by and nothing happened.

Meanwhile, Charlotte sent *Jane Eyre* off to Smith, Elder & Co.

Mr Smith, the publisher, began reading it on a Saturday.

He could not put the book down,
and cancelled his plans for Sunday
so that he could finish the book.

Smith, Elder & Co.,

Publishers,

Cornhill,

London

Dear Mr Currer Bell,

We are delighted to tell you that, having

read your manuscript, Jane Eyre, we

would like to publish it immediately.

Yours sincerely,

George Smith

Both Anne and Emily
congratulated Charlotte. Despite
being upset that their books were
not yet published, they were over
the moon for their older sister.
Six weeks later, in October 1847,
Charlotte received a copy of her
finished book, *Jane Eyre*. It was
perfect.

In December 1847, after months
of anxious waiting, Emily's and
Anne's books were finally published.
Both *Jane Eyre* and *Wuthering*

Heights were immediately
successful. George Smith, the
publisher, sent Charlotte many
reviews and articles about *Jane*

Eyre from the newspapers. After some very good reviews from some well-known writers, Charlotte decided that it was time to tell their father about her book. Patrick Brontë showed little surprise. He had often seen his daughters writing late into the night.

There was also much talk in the village of Haworth about who these three strange authors were. Nobody had ever heard of Currer, Ellis or Acton Bell before, but the postman often had to deliver mail for them at the Parsonage.

After much discussion, the three sisters decided to go to London and tell their publishers who they were. They were the authors of *Jane Eyre*, *Wuthering Heights* and *Agnes Grey* – and they were women.

Branwell's illness continued, until he eventually took to his bed. He died in September 1848, aged thirty-one, of tuberculosis.

The Parsonage, Haworth   October 1848

My dear Ellen,

All the days of this winter have gone darkly and heavily like a funeral train. We miss Branwell very much.

Since September, sickness has not left this house. Emily has a cough and a fever, and has become very thin. She is as dear to me as life. It is agony to watch her trying to breath.

Charlotte

Emily fought to continue on as normal for as long as she could. She struggled to dress herself and feed the dogs, gasping for breath all the time. Eventually she could not get out of her bed, and her beloved dog, Keeper, lay by her bedside constantly.

One December morning, Charlotte went out searching the moors for a sprig of heather to take to her sister. Emily loved those flowers dearly. Later that morning, she died in her sleep. The family buried Emily in the church. Keeper lay in a pew during the service and howled at Emily's bedroom door for a long time afterwards.

Chapter Ten

The following year, Charlotte's publisher, Smith & Elder, republished the sisters' book of poems as well as Anne's new novel, *The Tenant of Wildfell Hall*.

But Anne had become ill with tuberculosis, too. She began to yearn to visit Scarborough, where she had enjoyed holidays with the Robinsons as their governess.

The winter was harsh, and the Parsonage cold. Charlotte desperately hoped that the weather would improve and help Anne feel better, although she knew in her heart that it wouldn't make any difference.

The family made plans for Anne, Charlotte and Ellen to visit Scarborough. They all knew that Anne was going to die there.

Annc said sad goodbyes with her father and her beloved dog, Flossy.

In Scarborough, they rented a room looking out at the sea. Anne sat by the large window for the last couple of days of her life.

Charlotte wrote in her diary:

My poor sister, Anne, died on Monday evening (28th May 1849), aged twenty-nine. With almost her last breath she said she was happy.

Charlotte returned home in June. She was alone now, as she walked around the table each evening. There was no one left with whom to discuss her books.

She wrote to her friend Ellen:

When I arrived home Keeper and Flossy, Emily's and Anne's dogs, ran past me looking for my sisters.

I do not know how life will pass. The worst time is in the evening, when we would meet and talk. Now I sit by myself.

Charlotte found that writing was her best companion. She worked tirelessly on more novels, and in 1849 *Shirley* was published.

Sickness and death continued to plague the Parsonage. Patrick was often ill with bronchitis and Charlotte herself frequently suffered from toothache, headaches, colds and fevers. Then, in 1851, the Brontës suffered another family loss. Emily's dog, Keeper, died.

The Parsonage, Haworth   March 1851

Dear Ellen,

Poor old Keeper died last Monday morning; after being ill all night he went gently to sleep. We laid his old

faithful body in the garden. Flossy is
sad and misses him.
Charlotte

Meanwhile, Charlotte's career
had never been healthier. During
the couple of years since Anne's
death, her real name as an author
had become well known. She finally
had the recognition she deserved.

Chapter Eleven

One day, in December 1852, just before the publication of Charlotte's third novel, *Villette*, her father's curate, Arthur Bell Nicholls, proposed to her.

Charlotte, now a famous author, had earned fifteen hundred pounds from her books. This was far more than Arthur had, and Patrick Brontë believed that he only intended to marry Charlotte for her money. He told Arthur to never mention his daughter's name again.

Charlotte worried that her father was right. She did not love Arthur, and disagreed with him often. However, Charlotte had turned down three other proposals during her life already. She did not want to be alone.

After a while of not hearing from Charlotte, Arthur left for another position in a different parish. After a few weeks, Arthur started to write letters to Charlotte. She kept the letters secret from her father, and gradually the two grew to know one another. In the end, his patience and utter devotion to her succeeded. Charlotte agreed to meet him in the next village, and she could no longer deny that they were in love.

Summoning her courage, Charlotte told her father about her feelings for

Arthur. After a harsh wintcr, hc at
last agreed to their marriage and
reinstated Arthur as curate.

The Parsonage, Haworth   April 1854

My dear Ellen,

I am engaged to Arthur Nicholls! My
early dislike of him has grown, through
respect, to real affection.

    We are to be married on Thursday
29th June.

    You must be there with me, dear friend.

Love,

Charlotte

It was a small wedding with only a few guests. Miss Wooler, Charlotte's former teacher, gave her away, and Ellen was a witness. They spent their honeymoon visiting Arthur Nicholls' family in Ireland, with whom Charlotte got along very well.

Once they returned, they lived together in the Parsonage so that Charlotte could continue to look after her father. She was happier than she could have imagined. But her happiness was not to last long.

Soon after the wedding, Charlotte became pregnant and suffered greatly from severe morning sickness. During the brief times when she was not feeling sick, she loved to walk on her beloved moors.

During one such walk, she was caught in a rainstorm and fell even more ill.

The Parsonage, Haworth   February 1855

Dear Ellen,

My sufferings are very great, my nights indescribable. I have sickness without relief.

My husband is so tender, so good. I am thankful for him.

Charlotte

Charlotte and her unborn baby died in the early hours of Saturday, 31st March 1855, with her husband at her side. She was thirty-eight years old.

Patrick Brontë, now an old man, had outlived his wife and all his six children. He eventually died in 1861, aged eighty-five.

Arthur Bell Nicholls sold the Parsonage and returned to Ireland.

There were no Brontës left in Haworth.

Afterword

Charlotte, Emily and Anne were three incredible women who fought against all of the challenges they faced in their era. Now, over two centuries since the sisters lived, their books are still amongst the most popular in the world. They changed the course of English literature forever.

The sisters lived very restricted lives and were very private people. Despite their personality differences, they appeared to get on very well. Charlotte was strong and domineering, while Emily was incredibly shy and much preferred being with her animals over people. Anne was the gentlest of them all, yet she was also very determined.

The Brontë sisters lived exceptionally short lives, even considering the short life expectancy in their times. As well as their many sadnesses, it is obvious that they shared many moments of great happiness together and with their family, friends and pets.

The Parsonage is now a museum where the rooms have been furnished to look just as they would have in

the Brontës' day. Many artefacts
can be seen there, including some of
the letters the women wrote to one
another, as well as the tiny books
they wrote about their wonderful,
imaginary land of Angria.

I huddled against the rain-splattered window and looked out onto the grey, bleak moors. The wind howled and I shivered.

Plain and poor, Jane Eyre has always been treated unkindly. Her aunt and cousins despise her, and her school is cruel. One day, Jane sets out on her own to be a governess at Thornfield Hall. Here, Jane meets serious Mr Rochester, the master of the house. And there is a strange, eerie laughter coming from the attic …